the highest of all! (Plus or minus.)' Biblical resonance and legendary importance alike emerge here, as do meditations of pure lyric intensity and longing that take the reader deep into the joy and challenge of monastic life.

— *GLENN C. ARBERY PHD, President, Wyoming Catholic College*

This book of poems, fruit of contemplation of the monks of Silverstream Priory, is a gift. The pieces are variously traditional and penned by the brothers themselves. Most are evidently born of the deepest silence and prayer; some are written in fun and to entertain in Chestertonian style. All offer a privileged glimpse into a life lived close to God and steeped in the significance of language and beauty. Many of the pieces are akin to prayers and will be helpful in Adoration and the spiritual life of the reader. In short, this book allows us to become, in a small but rich sense, a part of the monks' way.

— *SALLY READ, author,* Night's Bright Darkness *and* Dawn of This Hunger

Only poetry can speak of what is beyond definition: it alone can convey an intuition of the opening to infinite mystery that is our life with the Lord. These poems express the unction of worship. They are deeply rooted in Scripture, liturgy and the lives of the saints, yet they transform the ordinary: 'Our world is magic in disguise,' they say. Playful and humorous, joyful and solemn, learned and peace-filled, they articulate life in a monastery. They speak of simply being friends with God, declaring, 'My coldness rejoices / In His warmth. / And so we are happy together.'

— *FATHER LUKE BELL OSB, author* The Mystery of Identity

DAWN TEARS,
SPRING LIGHT,
ROOD PEACE:
POEMS

Dawn Tears, Spring Light, Rood Peace

POEMS

BY MONKS OF SILVERSTREAM PRIORY

THE CENÁCLE PRESS
AT SILVERSTREAM PRIORY

The Cenacle Press at Silverstream Priory
Silverstream Priory
Stamullen, County Meath, K32 T189, Ireland
www.cenaclepress.com

ppr 978-1-915544-00-1
cloth 978-1-915544-01-8
ebook 978-1-915544-02-5

Book and cover design
by Michael Schrauzer
Cover art: Saint *Benedict in Prayer*
by a monk of Silverstream Priory,
modified by Michael Schrauzer

TABLE OF CONTENTS

AUTHORS' FOREWORD

THIS BOOK CONTAINS THE POETRY of several monks of Silverstream Priory. It invites the reader into a cloister of poems, there to look with eyes of faith through the arches of rhythm and rhyme onto the wide vistas, terrible chasms, and hazy mountains of Mystery, Beauty, and Love. Some poems let memory and imagination search the corners of the earth, there to glean the sorrows, hopes, and joys of men, and so present them to the Father. Others draw from the deep wells of tradition, with verse translations of ancient Latin hymns, or new compositions in that Catholic tongue. From there, gazing upwards, free verse explores the dark night of the soul, only to discover a sky star-speckled with the hope of immortality.

All the same, though the contemplation of Truth, Beauty, and Love is the characteristic work of the monk, one may be tempted to consider the peculiar fruits of these 'mental meanderings' as a misplaced use of time and energy for Benedictine Monks of Perpetual Adoration. It ought to be said, then, that these poems, whether written in darkness, light, or peace, in no way contravene our threefold vows. Rather, one could say that they assist one in living these vows — and in living our Holy Rule. Indeed, all three of the themes in this small book of poetry are found, perhaps ironically, in our Holy Father's chapter 'On the observance of Lent,' the spirit of which, according to St Benedict, ought to animate the monk at all times (cf. *Holy Rule*, ch. 49). Darkness turns to prayer (*orationes peculiares* or 'private prayers'); peace plants roots deep into the soil of the Divine Goodness, awaiting the Eternal Day 'with all spiritual longing'; and light bursts forth with the joy of the Holy Spirit either in thanksgiving or the sheer delight of the goodness of God and His creation. As the hymn at Monday Lauds puts it:

Christusque nobis sit cibus	So may Christ be food to us
Potusque noster sit fides;	Drink, too, may faith be;
Laeti bibamus sobriam	Joyful let us drink
Ebrietatem Spiritus.	The Spirit's sober ebriety.

Despite his cautioning against dissipation, St Benedict knows well that 'God loveth a cheerful giver' (2 Cor. 9:7; *Rule*, ch. 5). The Benedictine vows of Obedience, Stability, and Conversion of Life achieve their richest fulfilment in our union with the mystery of Christ's sacrifice upon the Cross, made present in every Holy Mass, and prolonged upon our altars in Eucharistic adoration. Our hope, then, is that as this book presents sparks of prayer, glimmers of light, and moments of laughter, it will carry to each reader something of the joy with which we run in all spiritual longing while we have the light of Christ (*Rule*, Prologue).

This is manifested in the themes of the three parts: Part I gathers poems that address themes of spiritual darkness, search, and self-gift. Its theme is represented by 'dawn tears.' Dawn is a time of transition; it contains both light (*The Secret of the Sacred Heart*) and darkness (*Prayer of the Senses*). Even if the darkness seems to dominate, however, one cannot call night dawn unless one knows the light exists. In opening with the *Stabat Mater*, we remind readers of the fact that, as Christians, we know that we are not alone in suffering, and that for us it even can have a redemptive finality.

Part II begins and ends with humorous poems about poetry itself. It contains both recreation poems composed for the celebration of various brothers' name days as well as more serious poems that exult in the beauty of nature and the economy of salvation (*Emitte Spiritum Tuum; Evelyn and the Dragon*). Here the silhouettes and hardly distinguishable shapes of dawn burgeon forth into a more certain and joyful spring. Though the transience of this life is not lost, it fades into the background as the light of life has its turn (cf. *Holy Rule*, Prologue). In this light, we seek to imitate Wisdom, playing before the Lord at all times (Prov. 8:30) and running in the sweetness of God's commandments so as to reach, at last, the heavenly fatherland (cf. *Holy Rule*, Prologue & ch. 72).

The third part is dedicated to the paradoxical theme of the spiritual peace brought by the cross. Opening with alternate verses of two favorite Christmas hymns, the poems of Part III portray the current of divine life conveyed to us through the Sacraments of the Church (*Pange Lingua*; *Fractio*). The witness of consecrated life is meditated in *Anno Domini 1880* and *Immortal Bride*. The created world also plays its role in communicating God to the soul (*Wyoming Dusk*) as does Sacred Scripture (*Mount Carmel*; *After God's Heart*).

The sections can be viewed from several angles. On one level, they move from time to eternity, from the created to the uncreated. Dawn is a daily beginning; spring, a yearly resurrection and transition; the cross, an eternal reality in which time is subsumed and redeemed. They also interweave the interior and subjective with the exterior and objective. Tears spring from what we experience; we perceive the exterior world by the created lights of the universe and are led into the eternal; supernatural peace drops down into our hearts and minds as a gift of God that surpasses nature, a result of God's redemptive realities.

While the poems were composed individually and without reference to each other, we have tried to arrange them such that they both complement each other thematically and provide stylistic variation. Their placement in the different sections can assist, and even influence, their interpretation. Thus, the silence in which *Conversation* ends should be read in the context of the peace of the whole third section,

while the whole book would be incomplete but for the
hope contained above all in the last lines of the final poem:

> *Coheirs and companions name us,*
> *In thy saints' high citadel.*

PART I
Tears in
the Dawn

1. Stabat Mater

There the mournful Mother stood,
Tearful by the Cross' wood,
While upon it hung her Son.

And her soul, immersed in weeping,
Deep in pain and sorrow steeping,
Through by Simeon's sword was run.

O how sad and sore afflicted,
She, of not one sin convicted,
With the Sole-Begotten crowned;

Paining, pining like no other,
As beheld the gentle Mother
Sufferings in her Child renowned.

Who is he who'd not weep with her,
Seeing Christ's own Mother, thither
Brought low by such heavy scourge?

Who is he, who, once considered
Son and Mother both embittered,
Could not feel deep pity's urge?

For the sins of His own nation,
'Neath the scourge's subjugation,
She saw Jesus' torment grave;

And she saw her Child tender
As an unconsoled offender
Dying, as His Ghost he gave.

Hear me Mother, loving fountain,
Make me seem His pains to count in,
That together we may dole.

Make my heart to burn with fervour
For Christ God, its one Deserver,
That the Same I may console.

Do this for me, Mother holy,
Pierce my heart and pierce it wholly
With the punctures of the Cross.

Of His pains, your wounded Child,
By the same for me defiled,
Let my share not suffer loss.

Make me weep with poignant feeling,
Thus the Crucified revealing
In myself, till I prevail.

Make me by the Cross keep vigil;
Seal me with your very sigil,
So I yearn, that I may wail.

Virgins of all virgins best,
With your sorrow fill my breast;
Unto me be not unsweet.

Christ in death grant me to bear,
Of His passion claim a share,
And its memory repeat.

Make me wounded with His gorings;
By the Cross to lose my moorings,
And the Son's Blood flowing fresh.

Lest the blazing fire burn me,
O Protectress, do not spurn me
When the wheat is put to thresh.

Christ, when I have journeyed hence,
Grant, by her, that I commence
Unto the palm, the vict'ry prize.

When death makes flesh no exception,
Grant the soul the sweet reception
Of Your glorious paradise.

Amen.

2. Dara's Darkness

See Sabine Baring-Gould's account of St Brigid's healing of the blind nun Dara. Finding her recollection disturbed, she asked for her blindness to be restored.

Come, sweet darkness,
Reveal again the Face
Incarnate of our race,
My Lover's only likeness.

Such gazing bids me bide,
Far from shining glade,
In wholly hallowed shade
Of Lover crucified.

Close again my sight,
O Mother mine,
By hand of thine,
From earthly light.

O my gentle sister,
With light so strong
My heart does long
For Bridegroom's whisper.

I see the rising mist,
A silver bright dawn;
But heaven's golden throng
I can no longer list.

Sun ascends mountains,
Throwing warmth across my face,
O, but sweeter is the grace
To drink at cloister fountains;

There comes one embrace;
There the Wounded of the lance
Sweeps you up in thorny dance,
And all the saints keep pace;

There the marv'ling stars
Are winding ceaseless praise,
And the Ancient of the Days
Has erased all their scars.

O song and dance,
O mystery mine;
My love Divine,
Contained within a glance.

Darkness, do thou then approach.
Come, wrap these eyes, all pale,
Take sight again, so frail:
I take thee without reproach.

Now I have Him fast,
I that am His likeness;
In the lightsome darkness,
We are one at last.

3. A Musician's Holocaust

Somewhere,
Lies a lute; for long, now, mute.
There is no sheen of finger-sweat upon the fret;
Dust dulls the rosette.
Now that the last echoes of the past
Have drifted into void,
There comes a still, small voice:

'My son,
Before I formed thee in the womb, I knew thee;
When thy little hands were empty,
And thy whole self wrapped in silence.
Let again thy hands hang idle,
Make no melody resound:
All the same, My own thou shalt be found.

I do not ask for merry tunes of England,
Or the filigree of Italy —
Are not all Mine the choirs nine divine?
And thy recordings are before me always.
I do not ask for strings of steel,
Or of the guts of cats;
This is My desire: the cords of human throats,
Spanning, not from nut to bridge,
But heart to mouth.

My son,
Give thy voice to My praise,
And I shall make of thee
A great nation.'

4. Three Years Later

To you, O Lord,
I bring silence,
Unwept tears.

An ocean, Lord,
Let me offer an
Ocean in silence.

My hands are empty,
My body still,
But my heart...

My heart?
What is, where is
My heart?

I come to you
Looking for it.
It was yours, long ago.

But I felt it, now,
Just a moment ago, and
It was not all yours.

5. Neminem viderunt nisi solum Jesum

I

1. Standing, prostrate, watchful, in sleep,
Constant his heart offers one plea:
'*Animam meam non exaltavi.*'
Yet my heart doth heavily heap
Arrogance, pride, and vanity.

2. Look I to a tree by weeds weighed,
Or a stock run red with bled beet,
Or spud sprung from earth, its white-fleshed
    meat,
Mixed with water crimson colour,
And say I can see Christ conveyed?

3. But, poor heart, how do I see Him
In tree, now free, or water run red,
Yet not in face nor eye nor limb?
Vanity, from it my eyes avert,
O Lord, teach me to look within.

4. For I see some eyes like fountains flow,
Others as though with fire aglow.
Each their own signs, but tell one tale.
Wherefore envy? Wherefore sorrow?
You too point; you differ, don't fail.

5. Could our father then be right?
Is all contained in one beam of light?
Listen, and then gain sight.
For there's but one story told
And each man must tell it bold.

6. The Apostle first saw it so:
Made man both poet and story

In one, summed up to God's glory.
'*Tunc dixi: ecce venio.*
All to this is allegory.'

7. A similar theme the Poet told:
'Christ plays in ten thousand places.'
But, to see Him in their faces,
First to Host attend, behold!
He their summary, make, and mould.

8. And these things are an allegory.
Of all, He is their summary.
Neminem videamus nisi solum Jesum.

II

Step by step away from the house I go
Towards the work obedience demands.
A tree waits at the end, was I to know?
Wrapped thick with thorns and thistles, silent
      stands.

Along the way my mind is back at home;
Heart hurting from moments with them unspent.
Heavy yoke, burden hard, I voice my groan:
'I thought union with You would pain relent.'

At that column, vine tougher than the rest
Forces me to ascend into the tree.
Pricked, pierced, battered, bruised, tattered
      from the test...
I submit, offer it for them and Thee.

Bittersweet the taste of His-my story.
'Offer, priest. It is the weight of glory.'

6. Reading Beside an Hourglass

Seconds pass, smooth sliding,
Sandy glass never restful biding,
Moves unchecked and grows,
Steady in the flawless flows.

Turning swift in space
The falling find their place,
Rising line, falling veil:
Such tells a deathly tale.

Closes now the river
In a gentle shiver;
There, a last dark grain,
Ceases all loss and gain.

Time made visible cries,
As within time flies:
I am time's icon.
Let not life pass on.

Beside me pages turn
All care for time they spurn,
Yet in my frame I feel
Naught that dalliance can heal.

Smooth sliding seconds pass
As slipping sand in hourglass.
Even so, world round,
A hundred thousand drifting souls are found.

Tumbling loose before the end,
If moments now they spend
Are gone in narrow strait,
What is their final state?

Of this I nothing know,
Yet watch I this gentle flow
And seeing the stream abate,
Pray that I may wasteless wait.

7. The Secret of the Sacred Heart

In a secret part of the Sacred Heart,
Behind the flames we know so well,
The flames consuming death and hell,
There lies a guarded mystery:

For at the cavern in His side
Whence ever rolls salvation's tide,
Two trickles, turning back inside,
Pursue their course in secrecy.

The first, the Blood, feeds in the furnace
Of His Heart to burn and burnish,
Souls to find and forge and furnish
With His sun-intenser love.

But the second, Water, beckons
Back beyond where man's eye reckons
As the Heart beats history's seconds,
Past the alcove-dwelling dove,

There, behind the wall of fire,
Hid from men's and devils' ire,
High cliffs gather and conspire
To conceal a sacred pool;

Here not light, but nightfall lovely,
Sub His *umbra* deepened doubly,
Ripple none, nor speak of bubbly;
Here not heat, but soothing cool.

On its crystal face reflected
All of Abram's stars, protected
By Him who has sole inflected
Each soul-child's secret name.

One brought there by Wisdom Holy,
Meek entreating, 'Mistress, show me,'
While the wade was yet below-knee
Heard, 'I make new, nor leave same...'

Then, the plunge
And sudden wake-up into long-forgotten dream,
Creation seems to stand, expand,
Astounding, bounding and resounding,
Filled with joy-life bursting into peace and I am
Free, all sight, no self, face forward arms flung
Backward, child's heart exulting, sculpting
      neverscapes come true,
I run them round and through;
All badness banished, batted back beyond
And never was, and never knew me,
Having been but born so newly;
Floating, drifting high upon His mercy-eye
And I its dapple-apple hanging on His tree
Rooted, grounded in charity no water quenches,
Like the dew it drenches fleece, behold the Lamb
Gives peace, and takes away the fray from day
      to day,
Deserve I? Nay, but say the word and I am cured;
He then descends into the cavern in my side,
Inside is heard as sung or sighed, not said,
Joining breast to loving head, and power
      reaching end
To end, as man to man and friend to friend
      confide,
'As I in thee, do ever thou in Me abide.'

8. Our Lady of Prompt Succour

Exsurgat Maria et dissipetur inimicus.
Knots they tighten, but plans unloose.
Et fugiant qui oderunt eam a facie ejus.
Crush their heads at last, untie the noose.

Maria mea in adjutorium inclina
They vent vile venom, yet without reason.
Domina mea ad adjuvandum festina.
Hasten to me as once to Judea.

Adjutrix mea, protectrix mea es tu
Against their plots, unceasingly new.
O Domina mea, adesto, neque moreris.
Delay no longer lest my soul perish.

'I am here.
My perpetual, prompt, powerful hand
Shall save you yet from their cruel band.
Cast your cares upon my pure heart
I'll nourish, save, and never depart.'

9. Matthew 19:29

I left them.
No longer are we near.

I seem to hear their conversation,
To see their faces.
But their voices are not there.
Their bodies, too, are distant.

Who is afar, them or I?
Who shall answer in this void?
Who will take my hand
And tell me how near this distance is?

In a snowstorm we lose sight of all,
Horizon, ground, and sky.
Is it light? Yes, for it is grey.
Is it dark? Yes, for it is grey.

Snowflakes blown diagonal the only bearing,
Slanting line the wind's apparition to the eye.
Distance ceases, now that here and there
Are hid in frost's erasure.

Blizzard's deathly blessing
Signs my face with cold
And every foot of world beyond my boots
Yields its mere existence to the past.

Not so now.
Distance here, and very close indeed,
Hurts and stings
With its insistence.

Like the snowflakes and my breath,
There and then clashes with here and now;
One must yield and melt
Or the other halt and freeze.

I have left them.
No longer are we near.
Breath of mine, shall you freeze
In past's embrace?

Or past, will you melt,
Water the soil of the present,
And give life unto my friend
The future?

Oh, I hear voices, I see faces, I feel hands.
Melt or freeze I must
Since distance will not cease.

10. Prayer of the Senses

When you love without word,
What can you say
When love must be worded?

O Word of Love, I love Thee;
Without words I wed Thee;
Without sound I hear Thee;
Without sight I see Thee;
Without knowledge I know Thee;
Without touch I feel Thee;
Without taste I savour Thee;
With love only do I love Thee.

Silence, I embrace Thee.
Blindness, I take Thee.
Ignorance, I accept Thee.
Numbness, I hold Thee.
Tastelessness, I receive Thee.
O Love, I receive, hold, accept, take, embrace Thee.

There are no words for this Word's Love;
There is only love for this Love's word.

I am all done. No more, no more.
Oh, begin now, begin. Increase, increase evermore.

11. November Second

As I walked over the ground,
Over the grass and muddy moss,
Above me whirled crow caw sound
And I thought of the loss
Around this world well wound.

Flying up the trunks of trees,
Diving through each laughing leaf,
My eyes plunged through the seas,
Over earth-bound bodies giving grief
When they alone are thought to please.

This ground here mellows,
All about me fallow flutters
In the wide-branched yellows
And the word-soft utters
Of wind-wild play-fellows.

Over the path our procession passes
And over the wind we wove mode flight,
Holding by a neum-borne pneuma fast
Darksome death's own frugal fright,
Its pointless presence pierced at last.

And I thought, 'One day I too shall lie,
In this same ground,
Under this same sky,
Without a sound,
Under these trees, high.'

Voiced in this same tone
By a generation unconceived,
Near these same stones,
I'll be sung for, unknown,
With the same songs I believed.

And I shall lie,
Beneath this same grass, green,
And these same stones, dry,
And all but I shall be seen,
And all but I, I, all but I
Shall be the same.

12. With Whom Shall I Watch?

Watch, because you know not what hour
your Lord will come (cf. Matt. 24).

Watch with that burning oil
    of the Virgins wise,
Watch with the housewife's
    lamp uplifted.
Watch with the hill-top city's
    tower guard.
Watch with the father of
    the prodigal son.
Watch with the hirelings
    looking for work.
Watch with the wise architect
    building on rock.
Watch with the lord of the harvest
    gathering cockle.
Watch with the rich king
    making a banquet.
Watch with poor Lazarus
    at the rich man's gate.
Watch with the woman
    seeking the coin.
Watch with the merchant man
    buying pearls.
Watch with the treasure hunter
    finding a field.
Watch with the king calculating
    treaties of peace.
Watch with the hypocrites
    surveying red skies.
Watch with the multitude
    strewing palm branches.

Watch with the traitor for
        the Master's morsel.
Watch with the sleepers
        in the dark garden.
Watch with the soldiers
        tossing their dice.
Watch with the guards
        at the tomb door.
Watch with the women
        on Easter morn.

Watch, because you know not
What hour your Lord will come.

13. The Preston Chantry

For ceaseless prayer they placed
Stones to house the humbled
Which godless henchman tumbled
And chantry walls effaced.

O speak, grey walls, do tell
What mysteries have you encased?
How rites within your precincts traced
Before your beams and lintels fell.

As frail man sought Redeemer's face,
What numberless neumes were laced
As priest to altar paced,
Christ on human hearts to place.

What were the vestments sewn
For olden Masses glorious
Invoking saints victorious
Before all ruin known?

Ruin now desolate stand!
Rubble of hallowed stone
All built for God alone,
Remnant of glorious Ireland.

14. Into the Desert at Night

There the dark is very dark,
And the stars are far away,
And the sand is bitter cold,
And the dunes are blue-black grey.

There the wind blows freely,
Rushes through the dry, silvered brush
On down, over the damp clay,
Across the waste, relentless in its push.

Star fades and the sky lightens,
Streak of pink, then heat's advance;
In blue so strong, light so crisp,
Waste is barren made in Sun's sure glance.

No sound but wind streaking sand,
No sight but hills' far distance
Quivering in heat-hazed dance,
Utter solitude's persistence.

Heart of mine, what have I to say?
Art thou dark but beautiful?
Soul of mine, is thy emptiness ready...
Ready for a presence true, a light immutable?

15. Purgatorio: Canto II

A NOVITIATE CLOTHING

Abyss. Gulf. Endless ocean. Angel ferry.
Turn your back;
Take those wandering souls on earthly shores.
You have disowned them;
Take them with.
But now they are utterly distant.

Heart on high;
Brace for the jolt of landing.
Ready the *tonus peregrinus* for perils ahead.
Dante's souls are chanting:
Yes, but they are saved.

Oh, father Abraham!
He cries across the gulf:
And even if I returned to tell them, they would not know,
They could not know;
Not until their soul sores are licked,
Not until they are nourished solely on their Master's crumbs,
Not until their feet are washed by Abbot's chrism'd hands...
O second baptism.

'Do not be afraid, it is I,'
Came through the scripture pages;
No, be not afraid.
This morning all is newly made.

16. Oblation

Crackling, consuming,
Glowing, dying,
Throbbing through strength,
Eating up weakness,
Sparks in the rushes,
Grass on the fire,
Heart hard pressed
In oblation's pyre.

For flowers of youth,
Cool streams of beauty
Splashing in maturity...
In their stead see now;
A forsaken waste,
Abandoned desert,
Arid plains,
An empty wild.

Will the desert blossom?
Will the fire fruit?
Will the ashes germinate
And the dust return life?
Will God accept my yes?

PART II

Light in the Spring

17. On Poetry

IN THE STYLE OF THE MAY MAGNIFICAT
BY GERARD MANLEY HOPKINS

Brother now turns twenty-four!
His birthday poem ought not to bore —
For like one eating curds and honey,
He knows gold from funny money!

But what, then, is in a poem?
Is a tome its only home?
What's the difference between verse,
And just prose that's merely terse?

Is it only that it rhymes,
Striking vowel sounds like chimes?
Must it always manage metre,
Paying Paul by pilf'ring Peter?

Ask him, the novice youngest —
He'll put his money where his tongue is...

Words are power, words are life,
With memory rife, and taste, and feel, and dream;
They breathe and heave or fly and float
Like *farfalline* on a summer breeze.

The secret song of highs and lows
In oo's and ah's and ee's and oh's;
A poet also must compose.

Chewy, crunchy, consonant clusters
Flip and fluster, twist and tease and tie the tongue —
That being sung,

Now paint and swirl a dreamworld
Only visible through child's eyes —
Divine surprise,
Our world is magic in disguise:

Smell the colours, see the sounds,
Like sweet perfume pink
And bright and shiny birdcall
Turning sunlight into song.

Forge new words, breed strange birds;
To bend and blend, combine, align and redesign
Is the fruition of a fertile intuition,
And an art, to speak the logic of the heart.

Let your rhyme replace your reason,
For all's well that ends by pleasin';
Highest treason, to sell freedom
For mere tedium.

Then, there's
Rhythm, a rollicking frolicking galloping stallion
Calms and flows and glides and slows unto a
Stop. Rests, breathes,
Lingers, ponders, tinkers,
Gaining speed he turns iambic and insists persists
        does not desist
Until he reach the end of each and every line —
Enough to sweetly daze, like wine.

'But friend,' you say,
'How can it ever end?'
One thing I've learned — if share I dare —
Is that you simply never know,
Until you're there.

18. Emitte Spiritum Tuum et Creabuntur

In rushing wind or silent breeze
Through field, meadow, or forest trees
I hear in part a song divine:
Kadosh, Kadosh, Kadosh.

From flapping finch to broad-winged crow
Their wings intone a hymn I know:
Therein I hear the Seraphs pray:
Kadosh, Kadosh, Kadosh.

In waterfall both large and small
Or crashing sea toss'd by the squall
A looking glass to heaven's throng:
Kadosh, Kadosh, Kadosh.

All earth desires to make it known,
With angel choir beneath the throne,
One over all is God alone:
Kadosh, Kadosh, Kadosh.

19. 'Pope' St Gregory VII

There once was a holy Toscano
Who was rightfully called 'Ildebrando'–
    For his name bears a flame,
    And his soul was the same:
He fought devilry mano-a-mano.

Oh, the Church was a mess when he reigned!
Of all vices she could have complained;
    Yet complain she did not,
    For her heart was a-rot,
So your pope said with fervour unfeigned:

'All of you who love sacrament-money,
Or the sweetness of lady-friend honey,
    Or by kings have been hired,
    Now listen — you're fired,
And don't think I'm try'na be funny!'

Then came Henry, his feet all a-frozen,
Saying, 'Father, repentance I've chosen!'
    The pope called from the window,
    'You don't look too thin, though!
That cowpie's still warm — stick your toes in!'

But Hank turned on him, wretch of a vassal,
And the pope had to flee to his castle;
    Then to Monte Cassino,
    And then to Salerno,
And suffered all manner of hassle.

Then he said, 'O my Lord, woe is me!'
And he sank on his bony old knee;
    'To be made such a pope
    Is the lot of a dope —
I should never have gone from Cluny!'

Then he stretched out his mercy's antenna:
'May God save all your souls from Gehenna!
    As I draw to a close,
    I forgive all my foes —
Save for Hank, and that fool from Ravenna!'

20. The Lay of King David

TO THE TUNE OF 'GREENSLEEVES'

Where Jesse dwelt went Samuel,
God's agéd prophet holy,
He said 'I seek the new king meek,
Thine ev'ry son now show me.
Nay, nay, again I say,
Hast thou no son besides these?'
'Yea, yea, in fields astray,
The least of sons of Jesse.'

Then in he came, of endless fame,
The humble shepherd David;
His ruddy face was full of grace,
Who Israël made savéd.
'Rise, rise!' said God the Lord,
'Let on his head the oil be poured.'
Hail, hail the new-made king!
'Tis David, son of Jesse.

Yet on the throne there sat alone
The former king of Judah:
His name was Saul, both strong and tall,
Yet weighed by spirit cruel.
Pain, pain assailed his brain,
A curse instead of blessing.
Who, who can cleanse him through,
But David, son of Jesse?

Then came the boy, the angels' joy,
To soothe his predecessor;
The truer king did play and sing,
The greater for the lesser.
Peace! Peace! The pain did cease,
Dispersed by lyre's sweet melody.

Praise, praise good Saul did raise,
For David, son of Jesse.

Then heathen men made war again—
So God His people trieth—
A Philistine was never seen
Like unto dread Goliath.
'Spear! Spear! Let him draw near,
The Jew who'd dare address me!'
Lo! Lo! The boy shall go,
Young David, son of Jesse.

On seeing him, Goliath grinned:
He bore no warrior-culture;
'Am I a dog thou think'st to flog?
Thy flesh shall feed the vulture!'
'Rise, rise, uncircumcised!
I need no arms to best thee:
God, God shall be my Rod!'
Said David, son of Jesse.

Then David ran to meet the man,
Five stones his only graces;
The giant loomed, the boy seemed doomed,
The Jew men hid their faces.
Fly! Fly! The stone sped by,
Straight in the forehead pressing:
Felled, felled the brute of hell,
By David, son of Jesse.

So every age shall know the page
Where David's life is written,
The shepherd meek whom God did seek,
Who left the giant smitten.
Play, play the psalmist's lay,
The Lord Most High confessing!
Sing, sing of God's own king,
Of David, son of Jesse!

21. Saint Thomas Aquinas

Let us sing of Saint Thomas Aquinas!
Of Church doctors he's surely the finest,
    For his score of IQ
    —If the rumour is true—
Was the highest of all! (Plus or minus.)

He was born in the town of Aquino,
And an oblate of Monte Cassino.
    While yet young it was known
    That his holiness shone,
Given neither to mischief nor *vino*.

A loose woman once gave him her *Sláinte*:
'Tommy boy, don't you know that I wancha?'
    But he ran to the fire'n
    Pulled out a hot iron,
And brandished it, shouting *'Sed contra!'*

Studying in the Order of Preachers,
Soon he bested the best of his teachers.
    Though to say it I hate,
    Listen, Albert the Great—
Think it's time to go sit in the bleachers.

What could ever compare with the Summa?
His an intellect fierce as a puma!
    And his thoughts on Our Lady—
    Though in one spot shady—
Say, *'Guarda che bella la luna!'*

Yet to show God's inscrutable ways:
When the priest made the last of his stays,
    It was not with his own ones,
    But Benedict's grandsons,
Cistercians, he ended his days.

22. Gudenberg

IN THE STYLE OF G.K. CHESTERTON'S 'LEPANTO'

Black crow caws from his perch atop the tree,
And he spies from on the mountain all the lands of Germany.
He can sense the growing danger to the shadow's tyranny:
And he caws at the encroaching Cross of Christianity.
Long ago, the southern Eagle thither spread unstable wings,
She was never wholly master of its chieftains and its kings;
Then her nest was sacked and burnt, and lost to men were
     many things—
But the crow grins to remember, he is cackling as he sings.

Yet the Eagle was a phoenix, it would seem, of olden time,
For she's burnt away the human and has put on the divine;
Now her vexsome old *vexilla* bear a new and strange design:
For the Cross of Christianity is marching on the Rhine.
But the barge of paganism is still far from being sunk;
Every Teuton has his idols round his neck and by his bunk,
And he labours up Mount Gudenberg to fall before the
     trunk—
(*Wynfrid at Exeter has just become a monk.*)

The Pope is on his balcony beneath the Roman sun:
She has ever shone the brighter since the ancient martyrs
     won;
She has seen the fall of Caesars and the routing of the Hun,
Yet within, without her borders dire cares are more than one:

Northern Europe lies in darkness (it lays thick upon Geismar);
To the east, Mohammed slaughters; at the gate is the Lombard;
Cries the Pope, 'O *Maris Stella*, lift aloft a shining star!'
(*Wynfrid of Exeter* introit ad altar'.)

In Friesland, old St Willibrord is kneeling as he prays,
And he casts a feeble eye upon his swiftly waning days:

'O my God, when shall the heathen here forsake his evil
    ways?
I have made my tears my bread; Thou gavest wine to us
    to daze.'

Lo! A Pentecostal spark now lights the Benedictine annal —
Lo! Our Lady lifts her foot the Midgard-serpent for to
    trammel —
  Holy Ghost ablaze! Huzzah!
  Domini Dextera!
  Wynfrid of Exeter
  Is sailing down the channel!

There's a psalter in his hands and grace is poured upon
    his mouth —
Wynfrid of Exeter is heading for the south!
Like a giant on his causeway, like the sun from out her house,
He is striding over Europe like a stallion on the joust.
On Mount Gudenberg, the priests of Thor climb up the
    craggy slope;
They have cruel knives and fire, they have victims on the rope,
And they pass beneath the oaken shade that blots all life
    and hope —
(Wynfrid of Exeter is speaking with the Pope.)

'Hail the wielder of *Mjölnir* and the lord of heaven's valves!'
Then the fire and the slaughter paint their desecrated albs,
And the tree drinks in the blood and takes the offering
    of scalps —
(Wynfrid — Ah, now Boniface! — has crossed the lower Alps!)
  Cross and crosier! Hip Hurrah!
  Sound the cry, Bavaria!
  Pray God gather all the Teutons in your young *Ecclesia!*
With the blessing of old Gregory, and the promise of Martel,
Boniface of Exeter has come to harrow hell!

Faster than the crow can fly he passes leagues no man can
     count —
Boniface of Exeter is making for the Mount —
And it cringes at his coming, shudders as he climbs the
     stones;
It convulses all the countryside, it rattles Radbod's bones.
Soon he scales Gudenberg unto its bitterest of peaks;
There is fire in the bishop's eyes, and frost upon his cheeks —
Lo, the oak! He stops, all's quiet. Then at last, the monster
     creaks,
Then it rustles, then it grumbles, then it growls, and it speaks:

'In Eden was a crow, who ate that old tree's rotting fruit;
Then my master bore him hence, that scattered seeds might
     take to root —
I am the son of Eden, and my roots reach down to hell;
The bane of all the living, whom no mortal man may fell!'

The bishop lifts his holy axe and makes the Signal of the
     Cross,
Then he rushes at the idol fleeter than a pebble's toss!
'Stroke the first is for the Father, who hath made the whole
     world good!'
The axe bites deeply in the trunk, and bark flies in his hood.

'Stroke the second is for Christ the Lord, who died upon
     the Tree!'
The boughs and branches hiss and moan, and blackened
     sap is spurting free.
'Stroke the third is for the Holy Ghost, the all-consuming
     fire!'
Now the terror of the Living God blots out the devil's ire.
     Hack and hew! Hullay Hulloo!
     Patris, Nati, Spiritus!
     Boniface of Exeter has cleft the monster through!

41

The old tree groans and bellows, roots wrench up from
      the abyss,
And its toppling is like thunder rolling off the precipice;
Its thousand-thousand demons shriek and cast about in
      vain for swine,
Then it crashes and they scatter all like ashes down the Rhine.
Since that fateful day, the Teuton priests have worn the
      Christian stole,
And the splinter of the idol has become the Church's pole.
All of Christendom rejoices every time the story's told:
For Boniface of Exeter has won the German soul!

23. St Aelred of Rievaulx

There once was an abbot of Rievaulx,
Whom I'll praise, if you'll pardon my drivels:
    For his life had no blame,
    And so holy his name,
When the devil's ear hears it, it shrivels.

It was Aelred, native of Hexham,
And the records — if ever you'll check some —
    Say he went to King David,
    That Scot surely savéd,
And never did ought that would vex 'im.

But he fled from the world for his God,
And returned to the old English sod,
    Then at Rievaulx met Bill,
    Who would teach him God's will
And the way of salvation to trod.

He held Jesus more precious than money,
And His holy Name sweeter than honey;
    When his love for Our Lord
    Through his pen was outpoured,
'Twas so ardent it's not even funny!

When at last in mortality's throes,
Filled with anguish from tonsure to toes,
    He said, 'Hasten, O death,
   Take away my last breath,
For I know where the love of Christ goes.'

24. Saints John Fisher and Thomas More

The two martyrs of June twenty-second
Are two Englishmen readily reckoned:
    They resisted the feds —
    Who made off with their heads —
And soon after to heaven were beckoned.

In Rochester, John Cardinal Fisher,
Who was never nor washy nor wishy-er,
    Told King Henry the Eighth:
    'Leave the lass, keep the faith,
Lest ye make in Christ's Body a fissure!'

Then your man, Thomas More, was the chancellor;
The oath rang, but he never did answer her;
    So they gave him the news
    That he'd sleep the great snooze
Once he cried, 'Conscience calls — I'll not cancel her!'

25. Evelyn and the Dragon

There once was princess Evelyn,
The daughter of a king;
She barefoot walked the forest floor,
And loved to dance and sing.
And wreathed around her golden hair,
A gift her father made and placéd there:
A crown of roses woven in a ring.

But once, she went a wand'ring where
No princess ought to go;
She carried past the warnings that
Her mem'ry tried to show,
And down the steep and stony vale
Where only shadows grow.

The serpent saw her. 'Lady fair!
Thou must have lost thy way,
Thy feet to grace this little vale
With precious little day!
Perhaps thou hast no homely house
Nor kindred with to stay?'

'Not so, for I am Evelyn,
The daughter of the king.
With him I want for nothing,
For I share in everything.'

'Alas, my lass,' the serpent hissed,
'I know thy father well,
And now I know that thou wert sent
So I the truth could tell.'
His tail flicked, his scales gleamed,
His eyes a-wove their spell.

'Thy father is a liar,
And thy soul he loveth not.
For all the world he'd not give share
Of anything he's got!
His only wish: to gain and hoard,
Though thy own flesh should rot.

'I counsel thee: put off that crown,
A collar fit for cattle,
And wanting only chain
To turn a princess into chattel!
Thy father's reign: an iron horse;
Thou nothing save the saddle.

'I do regret to give thee
Such a saddening surprise,
But it is only just that I
Should save thee from his lies.
And now, thy life is in thine hands:
So open up thine eyes!'

A moment stunned, but then she ran,
Hot tears upon her cheeks;
She ran and ran, not knowing where,
For hours, or days, or weeks;
And cast her crown upon the ground—
But where, no tale speaks.

At last, she found a tower tall
And shut herself inside.
'A curse upon my father's house,
Here only shall I bide!
My only friends, the cold and dark—
They only have not lied.'

The serpent followed. Seeing him,
'Come guard me in my castle!

Thy wage: to feast on all who come,
No matter lord or vassal!'

'My lady,' hissed the serpent,
'Both a privilege and delight!'
And so he prowled the tower round,
By day, and all the night;
With fuming breath he cursed the sun,
And blotted out its light.

But should the serpent fail —
Leaving nothing now to chance —
The princess, feeling restless,
Made provisions in advance:

She thought to draw the drawbridge up,
Then thinking crueller still,
She sabotaged the chains and beams
To fail their load, and kill.

And then, she set the seven vices
Hidden in the floor,
With iron teeth to clinch the legs
And revel in the gore.
Then, after greasing all the stairs,
She sealed her chamber door.

Now as the serpent, day by day,
Devoured man and beast,
He grew into a dragon
With his wings from west to east;
And plotted, in his wicked heart,
To make the girl his feast.

In time, there came Emmanuel,
The firstborn of the king;
A nobler man was never known,
And pure in everything.

He knew his sister Evelyn
Had sought the tower and locked herself within,
Sore wounded by an evil serpent's sting.

He made no show of splendour,
But became so very small,
That when the dragon crept around,
He noticed not at all.
And to the drawbridge drawing near,
By his humility he crossed it clear:
For he became so light as not to fall.

Then came the seven vices,
Set to stop him in his tracks;
But as he showed his mercy,
They began to show their cracks.
Then plying all his patience,
He with ease avoided all of their occasions:
For they became as soft as melted wax.

Then, persevering up the steps,
At last he reached her door.
He stopped—for though his power
Was a thousand times the more,
He would not break it down, as if
He were not come in peace to give a gift,
But rather robber come to plunder store.

'My sister! It is I,' he said,
'Emmanuel, thy brother.
Please open up to me—
I come in peace, and with no other.
I beg to have a word with thee,
Thy absence grieves my heart eternally;
I also bring thee news about our mother.'

The princess froze. Astonished
That he bested all her traps —
Nay, that he came at all,
Her withered heart could scarcely grasp:
Half screamed for him; the other rasped,
'Another trick, perhaps?'

'Thy father is a liar,
And our souls he loveth not.
Nor me nor thee would he give share
Of anything he's got.
And has he shown a single care,
While here I sit and rot?'

'O Evelyn,' her brother said,
'For this indeed I came:
We know that at the root of all
The serpent is to blame.
We long to have thee home again,
To dwell in light, and not this darkly den,
And put to death all memory of shame.'

Though warfare raged inside of her,
At length she loosed the latch:
Emmanuel appeared inside
Before her breath could catch.
'O Evelyn, how many years
I've longed to see this face, and dry its tears!'
He knelt, and reached for something from his satch.

But suddenly, the wall burst in,
Dust choked the princess' cries;
And in the breach, the dragon
Brought to bear his lidless eyes —
He gaped his horrid mouth's abyss
And moved to claim his prize!

49

But sword in hand, Emmanuel
Leapt in the dragon's maw;
He sliced its tongue, and broke its fangs,
And cracked apart its jaw.

Then, knowing what was coming,
Yet to consummate it fain,
He thrust his sword with all his might
Into the dragon's brain.

In wild rage, it thrashed and roared,
Careening earthen-bound,
Then burst in massive gusts of flame
Before it reached the ground.
'Emmanuel!' the princess cried,
And leaning through the gap, she strained and spied—
But neither ear nor eye could make him found.

In shock and swoon, she met the floor,
The ashes strewn like frost;
And lo, before her eyes,
The gift that now a life had cost:
The long-forgotten rosen crown,
As fresh as spring, and silken as a gown—
And not a single petal had been lost.

And down and down upon the crown
Ran rivers of her tears,
They ran and ran and washed away
The days and weeks and years;
And weeping on for time untold,
There came a sound, both beautiful and bold:
But hearing, she could not believe her ears.

She looked from out the wall again:
And there, afar below,
The king, her father, drawing near,

His horn aloft to blow.
And as it rang, the poisoned night
Broke up in clouds, and swiftly took its flight;
The golden rim of dawn began to glow.

The princess ran the whole way down,
No lightning half so fleet;
Not noticing her traps
Had disappeared beneath her feet.

'O father! O my father!
O, Emmanuel is dead!'
Her legs gave way, and slumping down
She sobbed and held her head.
But soon she felt her father's arms
Embrace, and magic-like erase her harms —
For twice as fast as hers his feet had sped.

'Thrice blesséd is the day when first
I saw thy infant face,
But thousand-fold the more when seen
Delivered from this place.
Would that the queen...' He silent fell.
'O father, is she well? Emmanuel...'
She stopped. 'My daughter, when thou left no trace,

At length, thy mother, sorrowing,
Took ill; at last, she died.
Since then, there's been no woman's heart
To govern at my side.
If thou accept, my Evelyn,
I would thee take thy place as next of kin,
And ever over all my realm abide.'

She could not speak. 'And also,
I would have thee understand,
That when thy brother died for thee,

It was as we had planned:
For none can conquer dragon-kind
Unless he leave his very life behind;
And so, he made thee heiress of the land.'

With trembling voice: 'When I am wed,
And my travail have done,
His name shall be upon my lips
When first I see my son.'
She offered him the crown,
And once again upon her head he set it down:
The new and endless era had begun.

When once again she'd walk the woods,
And dance, and freely sing,
From every hill and tree and vale
These words would clearly ring:

'All glory to the Father-King,
Whose name surpasseth worth,
And to his Son who gave his life
To grant the dead rebirth,
And to their Love that reigned between,
And turned a broken soul into a queen;
And this, in every age, throughout the earth.'

The End.

Amen. Alleluia!

26. St Dymphna

Saint Dymphna.
A nymph? Nah.
A pixi? *Non dixi.*
A Greek love? None to speak of.
A goddess? What oddness!
A saint? Do acquaint!
A martyr? Now you're hotter!
Irlandaise? So she says!
King's daughter? Now you've caught her!

St Dymphna, *ora pro nobis,*
We Irish Benedictine 'cenobies'!

27. For Brother Sacristan

Our sacristan is twenty-eight!
Must write a poem, and not too late!
But what does brother do,
When the Offices are through?

Does he slip on down to Whyte's
For a Guinness and some bites?
Does he hide out by the grotto,
Scratching tickets for the lotto?
At the last bell, does he risk it
Try to sneak in one last biscuit?

Ask the brother! He'll say, 'Well,
Only this much I can tell...

'Before the waking world can rise and sin,
The Lamb comes in; but first
He says, "I thirst." And so
The sparkling wine and water,
Finest wheat, I bring for slaughter.

'See the wax: I watch it wane,
As all day long they're slain, yet don't
complain;
Burnt not so much by fire as by Him
Whose love and ire
Singe the very Seraphim.

'Hallowed cloth and holy linen,
Shroud and winding-sheet and napkin
Pure and white; see now the Levite
Who with naked hand his naked Lord
Lays down on the unfolded swaddling band.

'Purple, green, and martyr's red,
Gold for glory, black for dead:
See them like the seasons stay,
Bloom and blossom; or within a single day
Pass on, and like old leaves be shed.

'Flowers snip and clip, at last they slip
In place, as though by grace,
Like angel choirs nine:
Order is divine.

'And brass, the humbler gold,
Must make to shine and flash as though
There's no such thing as old.
Mirror-silver, bright with fervour:
Gloves will serve her and the server.

'Then, when day shall finally falter,
Vesperal pall enrobes the altar —
Chant has lost her breath,
Sleeps, as though in death.

'In His chamber He retires,
Out go all the fires, save the lamp;
And now, the Lamb within
Awaits the morn, again to cleanse
The world of sin.'

28. On Limericks

So you've got your five lines, so ye do,
But they're not the same all the way through:
    For the third is quite short,
    And the fourth a retort,
But the length of the fifth should ring true.

You can start off with any old rhyme,
(Which for argument's sake we'll call 'prime')
    Then you bring in the second—
    Again swiftly reckoned—
Then chime the prime rhyme a third time.

Now the pacing does matter a bunch,
So take care that the rhythm don't hunch;
    The third line makes you feel
    Like you've slipped on a peel,
And the fifth takes you right to the punch.

Make it run, make it laugh, make it tickle;
And if ever you're caught in a pickle,
    Then do follow these rules
    Which are proven by fools—
Or if not, then just give it the sickle.

PART III

Peace
Before
the Rood

29. Verses for "O Come, O Come Emmanuel"

Veni, Veni Emmanuel,
Captivum solve Israël
Qui gemit in exilio,
Privatus Dei Filio.

Ŕ.: Gaude! Gaude! Emmanuel
Nascetur pro te, Israël.

Veni, Adam Novissime,
Per Unum vitam tríbue:
Et Fructum ventris Virginis
Suspende ligno sceleris. *Ŕ.*

Veni, O Abel Innocens,
Ovilem Deo offerens:
Peccata fratris ablue
In eloquente Sanguine. *Ŕ.*

Veni, O Noë Navifex:
Venite, dic, pusillus grex,
In Justi habitaculum,
Ne obruat diluvium. *Ŕ.*

Veni, Veni, Melchisedec,
Sine 'unde,' sine 'donec':
Da nobis panem caelicum,
Sacerdos in perpetuum. *Ŕ.*

Veni, Veni, O Isaac,
Et oves Agno salvos fac:
Qui prior eras Abrahae,
Ridens morte renascere. *Ŕ.*

Veni, Veni, O Moÿse,
Sub lege, ex muliere:
Duc ex Aegypto animas,
Et doce Dei semitas. ℟.

(For the feast of St Thomas,
21 December)

Veni, O Imago Dei:
Invisum profer visui,
Dexteram tuam digito,
Corque apertum dubio. ℟.

30. Verses for
"O Come, All Ye Faithful"
(BASED ON THE PROLOGUE OF ST. JOHN'S GOSPEL)

Adeste fideles laeti triumphantes,
Venite, venite in Bethlehem.
Natum videte
Regem angelorum:

℟.: *Venite adoremus (×3)*
Dominum.

Principio eras, Verbum apud Deum,
Et unum cum Deo Loquente es:
Teste Joanne, da Te cognoscamus. ℟.

Tu omnium Factor, hominumque Lumen,
Venisti, hunc mundum vivificans.
Mane in tuis: Te recipiemus. ℟.

Et non ex sanguinibus, neque mente carnis,
Jam neque ex voluntate hominum:
Solum ex Deo tibi sumus fratres. ℟.

Tu Deus aspectu panis involutus,
Mirabile nimis commercium:
Abiit panis, verbo Caro factus. ℟.

In fratribus Primo, et aeterno Patri:
Duobus cum obumbrante Spiritu
Omnis sit honor, gloriaque semper. ℟.

31. Sancte Joannes

Sitting in the boat —
Another day. Then, the Voice:
'Nets aside, and come!'

Cana, and the Pasch;
Tabor and Gethsemani;
'*Ecce Mater tua.*'

Joy when gapes the tomb,
Overshadows the Spirit,
Ascends God on high.

Newborn Church is weaned,
New Jerusalem awaits —
Eagle bright soars home.

Sancte Joannes, ora pro nobis.

32. Wyoming Dusk

Silk-green grey hush
Dusk-dark sage-brush
Over the plains.

Sand-stone dust drawn,
Lichen-lovely crunch crisp,
Over my hand.

Smooth purple-pink air
Far-floating deep there
Over the hills.

Quiet now, air wash,
Cold blue heaven's breeze,
Over my face.

Pried pine sap pungent
Sinks in the mountain murk
Over the wind.

Slime-splash, cool-laugh,
Water flows on clear,
Over the rocks.

You are there,
In sage-sand-pine air,
You are here, Lord, everywhere,
Over, overshadowing.

33. *Apocalypse* 14:13

As seraphim in gilded galleries,
I found an echo:
One beloved to another,
Vocem de coelo.

'Come apart,' the voice rang,
And I followed,
Into a desert place:
Dicentem mihi.

But I stopped to bring my coat,
Heedless of the word,
And in turning back,
Thought I pressed forward.

Already straight and clear,
A way in the wilderness:
'Plain to see and follow,'
Or so I said.

I plunged on, secure.
But in the arid heat,
Even the invincible are weak:
Beati mortui.

In the cold of night I froze,
The warm coat I stopped to wear
Turned to threadbare vices:
And so we perish.

In the desert I cried out,
But there is no appeal
For proud lips:
All their speech is vanity.

Like white bones picked by carion,
So my flesh faded.
As grass in a wildfire,
So my soul was brought to naught.

Even as a tree bereft of leaves,
My pride was revealed.
My thoughts, as branches,
Shown black, thin, and dry.

I could not move now:
And I did not.
I lay in the dust.
Memento homo, quia pulvis es.

Therefore, when I realised
That I could not go to His springs,
The beloved came to me,
Sicut dies verni.

He planted flowers,
And brought those springs,
Trickling, laughing sweet,
Jam hiems transiit.

He made the path straight,
Put tears in my eyes;
Together we drank from the laughing sweet
        springs;
And the desert blossomed.

I was now a child.
I had no voice to cry,
But He gave His words to me:
Let my cry come unto Thee.

And that I might stay and die,
A tower and a garden, a well within a wall:

These things he built for me:
Beati mortui.

With borrowed words I spoke:
De profundis clamavi,
And, casting off my coat:
Desiderio desideravi.

In that bliss-filled garden,
Labour and rest are one,
Sight and blindness look on God,
And heart is made whole when pierced.

Beati mortui, qui in Domino moriuntur.

34. Emicat Meridies

Noonday triumphs in the heavens,
Sabbaths seventy times seven,
For the maid Scholastica.

In the chambers penetrating,
Kisses from her one Spouse craving,
Loved with everlasting love.

Breath and death and sighs and groaning
Paid the maid, her hot heart glowing,
To obtain the better Part.

Heaven shuddered at her weeping,
And, in tears the whole world steeping,
She made soft her brother's heart.

In heaven, their conversation;
Benedict makes dissertation:
Saints' and angels' ecstasy.

Flesh and spirit sigh together
When her Builder who would wed her
Quickens her entirety.

'Come, thou lovely like no other,
Spouse and sister, bride and mother,
Come, receive thy destined crown.

'Mid the lilies take thy slumber,
Filled with pleasures passing number,
Deep in love to drink and drown.'

Dove of virgins, silver-bright wing,
On the riverbanks abiding,
Now you fly to glory's hall.

67

Draw us with your swoonsome fragrance,
Nurse us at the bosom stainless
Of God's grace, no more to fall.

Amen. Alleluia.

35. *Laeta Quies Magni Ducis*

SEQUENCE FOR THE FEAST OF SAINT BENEDICT

Joyful rest* for our great leader,
Gifts of light surpassing metre:
These the graces now renewed,

And to faithful spirits granted;
Let what openly is chanted
Vibrate hearts of fiery mood.

Marvel at the sight surprising
Of the patriarch arising
On this eastward-leading span.

Seed of seventy times seven,
Like unto the sun in heaven;
Very like to Abraham.

Mark the raven-servant pious—
In this recognise Elias,
Hiding in the little cave.

Elisaeus is detected
When the axe is resurrected
From the river's watery grave.

Joseph in his morals shining;
And, in future things divining,
Isaac's famous son we see.

May he, all his sons rememb'ring,
Bring us to the joys unending
Of Christ in eternity.

Amen. Alleluia.

*If not on 21 March: Day of joy

36. Mount Carmel

And Elias went up to the top of Carmel,
and casting himself upon the earth put his
face between his knees (3 Kings 18:42).

He felt the cool winds dry his sweat,
And stick his mantle to his back.
The last wisps of the holocaust
Confessed the glory of the God of Abraham,
The God of Isaac and the God of Jacob to his nostrils.
Below, he heard the faint but joyful *sonus epulantis*;
Then, he only heard the wind;
Then, just his breath.
And then,
A still, small voice:

'I am the Mother of knowledge and of fear,
Of fair love and of holy hope.
I am the barren who shall bear,
And in my womb is He who shall
Destroy the works of Baal
With the Holy Ghost, and fire.

He shall drop down like dew from heaven,
And with loud cries and with tears
He shall be heard;
The seas and winds — and rains — obey Him.

He shall be bread come from above,
On whose strength men shall be carried
Even to the holy mountain.

He shall be brought before all kings,
Who shall be shaken by the words
Of Him who opened not His mouth.

Upon His chosen He shall cast my scapular;
They shall leave all, give to the poor,
And take His sweet and gentle yoke.

And He the Son of me the Widow
Shall taste death, be overshadowed;
Then, upon the third time,
He shall rise again.

And you, my child, shall be His prophet,
And shall, even as myself,
Be borne aloft, both soul and body,
To the dwelling-place of God.'

And Elias said to his servant:
Ascende, et vide maria (Cf. 3 Kings 18:43).

37. De Amicitia or A Man Musing to His Friend

What is one flesh compared to one soul?
I in Him and He in me,
Is this not rather perfect charity?
But where do I attain this goal?

First: *Nisi cum,* no...
Nisi apud, no...
Nisi erat in nobis
We would know nought but the flood's flow.
Yet He is, I trust; only how so?

A different flood, in a way
More frightful than the first.
He pours Himself in flood,
Blood, to quench our thirst.

What? A mystery is this
More intimate than a kiss.
Why would vine Divine itself spend?
O bliss! Listen:
'I call you not servant, but friend.

'And friend entrusts to friend
Himself as though to himself.
At the last sup, see:
Take, all of you, for this is...Me.

'Yea, while servant, master, father, son
Are yet two,
The two are one
With friend to friend, with Me to you.'

Listen to that voice all ancient, shepherd-timbre,
    full-of-youth.
Has it not the ring of Truth?
Aye, I hear it there,
In that Reality to which we tend,
Where friend is oned with friend.

Yet outside the 'in', still there's more;
A face to which friends look, adore.
The truth with 'in' is so with 'to',
Since face 'to' face, we certain spy
Another self, apart, yet nigh.

Yes, friend is but mirror of friend,
Face but likeness of face
Veiled, even though in darkly manner.
For friendship reveals one from two,
As is with love, the form of virtue.

Now here we are, you and I,
So too a third, Christ, near by.
Friend to friend to friend,
Face to face to face,
He in me, in thee, and we in Him.

So here we reach our goal:
That union of soul to soul.
Whether face to face or within He be,
In this sweet truth lies all charity:
'I call you now friend.
To be alone I never did intend.'

Now here we are, both you and I,
And, I hope, a third. Christ,
The desire of our souls, fulfilled
In friendship that mystery divinely willed.

38. Simple Regard

In the grey mist
There is a golden light.
The mist is cold,
But the light is warm.
Near the warm light
The mist is also golden.
I am the grey mist.
God is the gold light.
My coldness rejoices
In His warmth.
And so we are happy together.

39. The Fourth Week of Lent

Glistening cantilena of notes,
Sweet cadence of eternity,
O light which flashing floats
In the silence of maternity.

O water washing stains,
Calling from a tomb
The first of many grains
To life within your womb.

You are the witness sure,
Beside the halted bier,
A searcher of the pure
Who stops to banish fear.

'Come to me, O blind,'
She cries within the light,
'And learn from panting hind
What waters give you sight.

'Magnify the mighty name,
And free for us the sound:
A love-song midst cloud-flame
When God His people found.'

Two women and a child,
One king and a sword,
God-man drives the wild,
Whips the temple's bestial horde.

Weeping woman shines,
Pit-stench banished, sees,
And man new mother finds
Adoring on his knees.

40. Vexilla Regis

The Kinges ensign sallieth forth,
The Roodes myst'ry radiance pour'th:
In flesh, the Same who flesh did make
Hath hung upon the double-stake.

Forsooth, thereon the Christ was pierc'd
By guardes lance-point fell and fierce;
That washéd be the world of sin
Flow'd blood and water from within.

Fulfilléd thus was everything
Fore-sung in psalm by David King,
Proclaiming: On all heathen sod
From on the Wood hath reignéd God!

O passing fair and radiant Tree,
Bedeck'd with Kinges purplery,
Whose choicest shaft was deeméd meet
Such hallow'd members for to greet.

Yea, happy: from the limbs thereof
This age's Ransom hung for love;
And, made His Body's balance-beam,
The daemon-hunted did redeem.

Hail, Holy Rood, sole hope of man!
Upon this Passiontides span,*
Make justice for the good to grow,
And to the guilty pardon show.

O God, Thou Highest Trinity,
Let every ghost give laud to Thee:

---

* *Outside of Passiontide:*
  Hail Holy Rood, hope else is none;
  By glory of the vict'ry won,

76

Whom by the Roodes mystery
Thou savest, rule eternally.

Amen.

41. Pange Lingua Gloriosi Prælium Certaminis (Crux Fidelis)

Sing, O tongue, sing of the glorious
Battle-contest full assailed,
And about the Cross victorious
Tell the noble triumph's tale:
How the world's Redeemer, for us
Immolated, yet prevailed.

When the Maker's firstmade, owing
All, yet grieved his God by theft
Of the fruit of evil knowing,
All were made of Life bereft;
For such debt, that tree was showing,
To the New was payment left.

In this work of our salvation,
As ordained by Providence,
Craft would foil his machination,
This world's shapeshift traitor-prince:
That, whence hostile degradation,
Balm thence for the ancient wince.

When, therefore, came the achieving
Of the longed-for sacred hour,
From the Father's bosom leaving:
Son, who made all things with power—
To the Virgin's womb now cleaving,
Robed in flesh: His Mother's dower.

Lo, inside the narrow manger,
Hear the Newborn feebly bleat;
Virgin Mother keeps from danger
Limbs within the swaddle's pleat;

Strictly binds the kind arranger
Hand, and legs, and little feet.

Fifth-year off'rings six completed,
Days of flesh gone like a dream;
He chose death, will-unimpeded,
Born for this alone: redeem.
On the Cross the Lamb is seated,
To be slain upon the beam.

See the reed, the gall, the spittle,
Vinegar and spikes and spear;
When they pierce the ribcage brittle
Blood and water both appear;
Sea, land, sky, and world so little
Drink the draught as thirsting deer.

Faithful Cross, whom all earth hails
As the only noble Tree!
For no forest aught prevails
Branch or bloom or bud o'er Thee!
Sweet the wood and sweet the nails
Charged with such sweet Gravity!

Bend thy boughs, O Tree exalted!
Grant the Flesh outstretched respite!
Let thy strength for Him be faulted,
Though, through nature, thine by right;
And Who rules the heavens vaulted:
Tend His limbs not overtight.

Thou alone wert worthy counted
As to bear the Price of all,
Ark and Harbour for the drownéd
World, in shipwreck since the Fall;

Priest-and-Lamb anointed, crownéd
Thee with Blood, as preacheth Paul.

Glory, honour be forever
Unto Thee, O God Most High:
Father, Son, united ever
In the Spirit whom They sigh;
Power, praise shall leave Them never,
Through the age that does not die.

Amen.

42. Saint Dunstan

He took harp,
Golden hum.
Struck firestrings
Tingle sharp
And speak the day's viaticum.

Dappled streams
Blossoming
Christendom
In my dreams,
Before he fades in my waking.

Harper saint,
Stay awhile
Banishing
Our complaint:
Teach us a song for this Isle.

43. Anno Domini 1880

1. SAINT ELIZABETH OF THE TRINITY
(1880–1906)

Beth, Sabeth, Elizabeth:
Don't cry, be still now.
It's thy six-and-twentieth.

Carmel's brown grace still endow
Gladly, laboureth
Deathly winnowing somehow.

Beth, Sabeth, Elizabeth!
Pure as blood thy vow,
Light, Love, Life, thy treasure-breath.

2. BLESSED ILDEFONSE SCHUSTER
(1880–1954)

Blessed Benedict's child,
Toil before sunset,
Thy cares parchment piled.

Shepherd shoulders his wet net:
With faith's guards beguiled,
He preserves prayer's alphabet.

I address thee, bishop mild,
Interceding yet,
Thy faith grant us undefiled.

44. Curramus

Across the ages the fleet foot's heard,
Much like a heart-beat, undeterred.

First the Virgin hast'ning to the hills,
Then the Holy Family from the babies' shrills.
Next, in the sweetness of her ointments from the tomb,
Magdalene pulls two friends from the upper room.

To and fro, back and forth, they run for all it's worth
To find the One to grant them everlasting birth.

Through the ages feet fall, though now along the way of
        God's commands,
And match the heart's pitter as they patter down the lane:
Benedict, Bernard, Gertrude, that and many more a name.
They step and stride and run along
To match Christ's heart-begotten song.

Further up and further in! We run as if to win
The prize that we've been promised: it waits at life's last Inn.

And you, my friend, are like them all.
You've heard the heart-string's call
That pulls you on and gives you life
Through weakness, dark, and strife.

The mockers mock and say: 'Your help is from above?'
'Yes,' you reply, 'and like hart, or rock-cleft dove,
I festinate for Crist luv.'

45. Immortal Bride

Blurred from time,
Speckled and torn,
Black and white line,
Photograph's young faces.

Framed by a veil
I see deep eyes;
Cloister in greyscale
Captured long ago.

She, like a friend,
Or as one once seen.
Another I would have liked to know;
But they are lost to us.

Now, what could I mark
Or find but birth dates,
A parish record faded,
And a few old archives?

Lost, all, are countless hours,
Deep sorrows, then joy,
And finally, peace.
They were real.

But to us, what are they?
And what has lasted
Of a human life
In one grey century?

Hid, all: all hid in God,
Her labours come and gone.
Perhaps we do not see
That lovers' garden dawn.

To this orchard of delights,
Hours, days, and months as naught;
Unsought are years and even life,
When priceless pearl is bought.

Once peering through the lattice,
Before her body whole was spent,
Lover's face no longer glimpsed
Since earthly veil is rent.

Her blindness given vision
As the finite photo fades,
She may not be so distant
When humbled hearts she aids.

United by the same,
Our father's single aim,
Blessed by grace and name:
It's for his Rule we came.

Though here forgotten,
She, immortal bride, remembers,
And with the Sole-begotten,
Sustains the Mystic Body's members.

46. Our Lady of the Cenacle

After Christ had ascended to heaven,
To the Cenacle, with the Eleven,
    Our Lady did go,
    And her presence did show
That among the new dough, she was leaven.

'*Ambulate*, my sons,' she did say,
'For alone I am left all the day.
    But do be of good cheer,
    For the Lord God is near,
And your prayers He shall hear on that day.

'Now the scent of my nard is arising,
In itself all your own prayers comprising;
    In the Cenacle stay,
    Do ye watch, do ye pray,
Till ye see what my Son is devising.'

'*Expectavi expectans*,' she said,
'And on Thee have I mused from my bed.
    Do Thou hasten, O Lord,
    On the leg gird Thy sword,
Let the Spirit be poured, and us wed.

'O virginity's lily and laurel,
Who my womb in Thy shade made Thy portal,
    Overshadow again,
    Gift of God unto men!
May the Cenacle's sons be immortal!'

47. Veni Creator Spiritus

Creator Spirit, now descend,
Greet inwardly Thy every friend;
Let flood Thy wing-beat wind of grace
Each fashioned heart and handmade face.

Well art Thou called the Paraclete,
Gift of the God whom no heights meet,
And Fire, and Love, and Fount alive,
And Unction making souls to thrive.

'Neath seven species come Thy gifts,
Thou finger whom God's right hand lifts;
The Father's solemn surety
Of Babel's purged impurity.

Ignite Thy light in every sense;
In hearts, Thy charity's incense,
To gird our weak, unwilling flesh
With Thine own power, ever fresh.

Beat back the foe of God and man,
Grant peace as naught of this world can:
With Thee as leader at the helm,
No evil thing shall overwhelm.

Grant us to know our Father great,
His Son's friendship to cultivate;
In Thee, Their life-breath doubly sighed,
May evermore our faith abide.

To Abba Father endless praise,
And Jesus Lord, whom He did raise
From death; and to the Paraclete,
Whose age an end shall never meet.

Amen. Alleluia.

48. Fractio

Silent bends the mantled man,
Settled on the sacred stone,
Folded in the Supper's sway,
God's Word is voiced by human's groan.

Heaves he higher still,
The orb of Wafer whiteness,
A globe of Deity incarnate,
A dark world's only brightness.

In mystic gesture's secret pleading
A hush enfolds the human way,
While, face to face with God, heart speeding,
I senseless gasp and say:

'Look Thou, O God, upon this Disk,
The which, upheld, I fear,
And free me of this folly,
That cannot see my Saviour here.'

Sinks now the leaf-like Morsel,
Shifting in the hallowed hand;
Lies now upon the winding sheet
Most priceless pearl of all the land.

Here heart-words hide,
Beyond the shriek of speech,
Silent in the deafening song
Of Love's enfolding reach.

Swept up again in faith's fair symbol,
Crossing ruddy ocean's deep,
Now riven in the fraction rite
As heaven's joy we keep.

The broken circle falls on gold,
In Blood's deep cup a Fragment rests;
Two halves infinity remain,
God come to His banquet-guests.

49. Conversation

A Face.
'A face?'
I have seen many faces.

There was, once,
One Face.
'There are many faces.'

I remember...
'— you remember
Many faces.'

No, there was one —
'Here is one.'
— No, not her.

'Or this one?'
— No, not him.
'Or this one?'

There was one,
'— one face?'
One Face.

'Whose face?'
God's Face.
'Not God's face.'

Yes. His.
'He doesn't have one.'
I saw it.

'You imagined it.'
A Face? Imagined?
'Yes. His.'

No.
There was a Face,
Yes, among many, one.

All others faded, then...
'— Long ago!'
Long ago.

'And now this one;
It too fades?'
Yes...

'Ah, yes.'
Ah, no, but you are
Veiled, my Jesus.

50. After God's Heart

So I turned, to see what voice it was that
was speaking to me... (Apoc. 1:12).

David:
Your eye is sharp, your ear is keen,
Has it not been sweet this grace?
I asked it for you, son of thunder,
To finish the image I traced.

All that I heard from afar
Or saw through veiled lens,
You by grace beheld
And learn by experience.

But this in common did He give:
An ear to His heart, by which we lived.

I — IN PRINCIPIO

By His Word the heavens were made!
From them His mercy flowed down.
To write this truth was my trade,
For, like love-struck boy of tender age,
Unto eternity I sang their renown.

But you, my son, what blessing is yours!
When Word dropped down and Truth revealed
That which my life only concealed.

You saw Him in the flesh,
And spoke to Him face to face;
You listened to His voice
So tender, so loving, so guileless,
And full of grace.

Ah! His face — what lovelier sight than this?
His visage, giving joy to friends;
Countenance, satisfying the heart within.
He sealed upon me the light therein.

I asked Him but one thing, that was my content.
'Your face, O Lord, my heart it seeks,
Lustering, lightening, calming, fighting:
This is my one request.'

'One alone?' said He, 'no, twice I have to give.
From you My face will not depart,
But incline more closely,
Listen to my all-thoughtful heart.

It waits betrayed, forgotten, lost,
For hearts as yours not cooled by frost.
And though it looks to friends for joys
It finds no soul that love employs.
But even so I pour love out;
How can I not for men without?
I love men dearly, they are Mine:
Created sign of Son divine.'

Thus, though I asked for His face,
His heart He gave me too,
That heart which you know well,
To which you listened,
And there did dwell.

III — *PANIS PINGUIS*

From face of light and heart of love
We were given to learn true life.
From its fountain something flowed:

Food to strengthen ways,
Draught to lengthen days
For the journey through death-valley's strife.

Bread of Angels! How I longed to taste,
See.
The sea of love that it contained,
Taste you did, and drink it too.
Waters fresh, wine of life —
Memorial and presence He left to you.

IV — *IN NOCTE*

But that gift came at a cost.
Though I nothing envy,

This more
Than the rest:
You were there when He, upon the tree,
Fully free
Did plea
Eli!
Eli!
Lama
Sabachthani!
My spirit I give to Thee.

Then more you saw — pure heart, sword-pierced —
And more you heard: the Mother of the Maccabee,
In sobs,
In whispers:
Viriliter age,
Viriliter age...

From the depths you cried:
'Lord, mine ear inclined,
What of Yours?!

I wait,
I wait before You at mercy's doors.
When shall it open? When...'

V — *IN FINEM*

John:
My lord and my king! Beautiful to behold!
From you I learned to listen.
That heart I love, I knew its sound
For you had taught me to listen.

Might you gave me in the darkness
When night seemed to have won.
I fixed my gaze and heard the words
You uttered about Mother and Son:

'Behold we heard in Ephrata,
We found in the place of the wood,
We entered into His tabernacle,
We adored where God's feet had stood.
Arise, O Lord, from Your test
Unto Your endless rest!'

As for what's left, good king, what of the Ark?
Please, to my Mother hark
And tell her: your son awaits!
His sojourn has been prolonged.
Bring me home to thee
For to thee and thy Son I belong.'

But the king did not respond.
He merely smiled and turned.
Then, though once came sound,
'Twas twice I heard.
Two voices, Son's by Mother's wound:

'My son, your time draws near.
Of what you see and have seen,
Of what you hear and have heard,
This is your final task:
Write to them of the Word.'

*And as I turned, I saw seven golden candlesticks, and
in the midst of these seven golden candlesticks one
who seemed like the Son of Man (Apoc. 1:13).*

51. Lauda Sion

Sing praise, Sion, to thy Saviour,
Praise thy Leader, Shepherd, Maker,
In hymns and in songs of love.

What thou mayest, so much dare thou;
For no laud can ought compare now,
Nor canst ever laud enough.

This the special theme for praising:
Bread alive to life a-raising,
This today we preach about.

That, at table laid by heaven,
To the crowd of His twelve brethren
It was given, none can doubt.

Be praise full and full-resounding,
Be it comely, charm-abounding,
In the mind's high gaiety.

For this day is held a solemn feasting,
When is put to memory unceasing
That first sup of Deity.

At this table of the new King,
Is the new Pasch of new ord'ring,
Elder days now meet their end.

Ancientness from novelty,
Shadows from the truth now flee,
Light the nightsome darkness fends.

What at supper Christ impresséd,
In the doing thus expresséd:
Evermore to venerate.

Lore of sacred service sav'ring,
Bread and wine into the saving
Victim now we consecrate.

This the dogma taught to Christians:
Bread to Flesh makes its submission,
And the wine to Precious Blood.

What thou graspest not nor seest,
Lively faith affirms the freest,
Soaring o'er confusion's flood.

Here, 'neath eyesight's meagre measure
Lies the heart of heaven's Treasure,
But the signs are all we find.

Flesh for food, and Blood for drinking,
Christ remaineth, past all thinking,
Whole and one beneath each kind.

In the taking is no rending,
Nor dividing, breaking, bending;
Sound and single Christ is had.

Taketh one and take a thousand;
One and all alike are houseled,
Nor the measure overspanned.

Take the good and take the evil;
Yet behold, what lots unequal:
Unto life, or unto death.

Death for wicked, life for good men:
Seeming same the sup in man's ken;
Yet how great the chasm's breadth.

When the Sacrament is broken,
Doubt not — think thou what was spoken:
Now is sundered but the token;
Beareth every bit the whole.

Matter none shall suffer tearing;
Signs are ruptured, substance sparing,
For nor state nor very being
Shall let spending take its toll.

Lo! Behold the bread of angels,
Made the bread of pilgrims, strangers;
Child's bread that no dog endangers,
Nor would dare his paw to lift.

In figures fore-indicated:
When Isaac is immolated;
Paschal Lamb is implicated;
Fathers take the manna-gift.

O Good Shepherd, Thou true Manna,
Jesus, save us from Gehenna:
Do Thou guide us, do Thou guard us;
Show us what shall never harm us,
There where life's end none may tell.

Thou, who knowest all and weighest,
Thou who feed'st us mortals greyest,
For thy holy ones do claim us,
Coheirs and companions name us,
In thy saints' high citadel.

Amen. Alleluia.

NOTES AND
TRANSLATIONS

All translations of text from Scripture are taken from the Douay-Rheims translation. The titles of books in the Bible and verse numberings accord with the titles and numbering of the Douay-Rheims.

5. NEMINEM VIDERUNT NISI JESUM —
AND THEY SAW NO ONE BUT JESUS (MATT. 17.8)

Animam meam non exaltavi — I have not exalted my soul (Ps. 130.1).

Tunc dixi: ecce venio — Then I said: behold, I come (Ps. 39.8, Heb. 10.7).

Neminem videamus nisi solum Jesum — Let us see no one but Jesus alone (Cf. Matt. 17.8).

7. THE SECRET OF THE SACRED HEART

Sub His umbra — Under His shadow (Cant. 2.3).

8. OUR LADY OF PROMPT SUCCOUR

Each Latin phrase is taken from the psalms and adapted to refer to our Lady. This is an idea found in St Bonaventure's Marian Psalter from the 13th century.

Exsurgat Maria et dissipetur inimicus — Let Mary arise and let the enemy be scattered (Ps. 67.1).

Et fugiant qui oderunt eam a facie ejus — And let those who hate her flee from before her face (Ps. 67.1).

Maria mea in adjutorium inclina — O My Mary, incline unto my aid (Ps. 69.1).

Domina mea ad adjuvandum festina — O My Lady, hasten to assist (Ps. 69.1).

Adjutrix mea, protectrix mea es tu — My helper, my protector art thou (Ps. 39.18).

Domina mea, adesto, neque moreris — O My Lady, come, and do not delay (Ps. 69.6, 39.18).

15. PURGATORIO: CANTO II

Tonus peregrinus — *the wandering tone.* This is one of the tones used for psalmody in the Divine Office; it is supposed by certain scholars to be a remnant of an ancient Jewish melody.

18. *EMITTE SPIRITUM TUUM ET CREABUNTUR*

The title of this poem translates to: *Send forth thy Spirit and they shall be created (Ps. 103.30).* It is part of a versicle for the feast of Pentecost. *Kadosh* is the Hebrew word for 'holy.' Hence, '*Kadosh, kadosh, kadosh,*' is the angelic hymn: 'Holy, Holy, Holy' mentioned both in the Prophecy of Isaias (Isa. 6.8) and the Apocalypse of St John (Apoc. 4.3).

19. POPE ST GREGORY VII

The final verse refers to Guibert of Ravenna, Antipope Clement III, elected in opposition to Gregory VII in 1080.

21. SAINT THOMAS AQUINAS

Sláinte is a common drinking toast in Irish.
Guarda che bella la luna! — *See how beautiful the moon!*

22. GUDENBERG

The poem is an imaginative account of St Boniface's felling of the Oak of Thor on Mount Gudenberg in modern-day Germany.

Vexilla — *banners*

Maris stella — *Star of the sea; Introit ad altar* — *he enters unto the altar (Cf. Ps. 42.4).* This psalm is used in the prayers at the foot of the altar in the *Usus Antiquior* of the Roman Rite.

Dextera Domini — *The right hand of the Lord (Ps. 117.16).*

Mjölnir — The mythical hammer of Thor

Ecclesia — *church*

Martel — Charles Martel, grandfather of Charlemagne, Duke and Prince of the Franks from 718-741.

Radbod — (also Redbad) anti-Christian duke of the Frisians, whose death in 719 paved the way for St Boniface's missionary efforts.

Patris, Nati, Spiritus — *Of the Father, of the Son, of the Spirit*

23. ST AELRED OF RIEVAULX

Rievaulx — traditionally pronounced 'Rivels'
Bill — Abbot William, first abbot of Rievaulx (1132-45)

25. EVELYN AND THE DRAGON

The length of stanzas having either six or seven lines bears numerological significance.

26. ST DYMPHNA

Non dixi — *I did not say*
Irlandaise — *Irish*
Ora pro nobis — *Pray for us*
Cenobies — *cenobites* (i.e. monks who live in community)

29. VERSES FOR *O COME, O COME EMMANUEL*

Come, Last Adam,
Through one Man grant life:
And the Fruit of the Virgin's womb
Hang upon the tree of the crime.

℟. Rejoice! Rejoice! Emmanuel
Shall come to you, O Israel.

Come, O Innocent Abel,
Offering the sheepfold to God:
Wash away the sins of the brother
In the eloquent Blood. ℟.

Come, O Noah Shipbuilder,
Say, 'Come, little flock,
Into the dwelling of the Just One,
Lest the flood overcome. ℟.

Come, Come, Melchizedek,
Without 'whence', without 'until':
Give us the heavenly bread,
Priest unto eternity. ℟.

Come, Come, O Isaac,
And by the Lamb save the sheep;
You who were before Abraham,
Laughing, be reborn through death. ℟.

Come, Come, O Moses,
Under the law, of woman:
Lead souls out of Egypt,
And teach the paths of God. ℟.

Come, O Image of God:
Bring forth the unseen to sight,
Your right hand to the finger,
And your open Heart to the doubtful. ℟.

30. VERSES FOR *O COME, ALL YE FAITHFUL*

Come, faithful ones, joyful, triumphant,
Come, come to Bethlehem.
Behold the Babe,
The King of angels.

℟.: *O Come, let us adore (x3)*
The Lord.

You were in the beginning, the Word with God,
And You are one with the God who speaks:
With John as witness, give us to know You. ℟.

You, the Maker of all, and the Light of men,
You came, giving life to this world.
Remain among Your own: we shall receive You. ℟.

And not from blood, nor the will of the flesh,
Nor indeed from the will of man:
Only from God are we brothers to You. ℟.

You are God wrapped in the appearance of bread,
O utterly wonderful exchange:
Bread has passed away, made Flesh by the word. ℟.

To the First among brothers, and to the Eternal Father:
To the Two, with the overshadowing Spirit,
Be all honour, and glory forever. ℟.

31. SANCTE JOANNES — ST JOHN
Ecce Mater tua — Behold your Mother (John 19.27).
Sancte Joannes, ora pro nobis — St John, pray for us.

33. APOCALYPSE 14:13

Vocem de caelo — The voice from heaven (Apoc. 14.13).

Dicentem mihi — [The voice from heaven] Speaking to me (Apoc. 14.13).

Beati mortui — Blessed are the deceased (Apoc. 14.13).

Memento homo, quia pulvis es — Remember man that thou art dust. This is said during the imposition of the ashes on Ash Wednesday and is taken from Genesis 3.19.

Sicut dies verni — As days of spring. This is taken from a Matins responsory for the Feast of the Assumption.

Jam hiems transiit — For the winter has passed (Cant. 2.11).

Beati mortui — Blessed are the deceased (Apoc. 14.13).

Desiderio desideravi — With desire have I desired (Luke 22.15); *De profundis clamavi* — From the depths have I cried (Ps. 129.1).

Beati mortui, qui in Domino moriuntur — Blessed are the deceased who have died in the Lord (Apoc. 14.13).

36. MOUNT CARMEL

Sonus epulantis — the sound of feasting (Ps. 41:5)

The final verse is an adaptation of the Vulgate, which reads: *Ascende, et prospice contra mare* — Arise, and look towards the sea (3 Kings 18.43).

37. DE AMICITIA OR A MAN MUSING TO HIS FRIEND

Nisi cum — Unless with

Nisi apud — Unless among

Nisi erat in nobis — Unless he were in us (Ps. 123.1).

39. THE FOURTH WEEK OF LENT

See the propers for the *Usus Antiquior* of Roman Rite in the Fourth Week of Lent. This poem comments on them in reverse order, i.e. it begins with the Saturday of the Fourth Week and traverses the week back to the Fourth Sunday of Lent.

41. PANGE LINGUA GLORIOSI PROELIUM CERTAMINIS

Lustris sex qui jam peractis is translated as 'Fifth-year off'rings six completed' (stanza 6). A *lustrum* was a Roman sacrifice offered every five years. Many translations of this hymn simply say 'thirty years', which both misses the sacrificial nuance and is inaccurate; Christ was crucified within the sixth *lustrum* of His lifetime.

44. CURRAMUS — LET US RUN

St Aelred of Rievaulx's last words were reputed to be: '*I festinate for Crist luv*' — *I hasten for the love of Christ*. According to St Aelred's disciple and biographer, Walter Daniel, St Aelred found that saying the Lord's name was 'easier to utter' and 'sweeter to hear' in his native tongue than in Latin. The Middle English spelling is retained in the poem.

46. OUR LADY OF THE CENACLE
Ambulate — *Walk (Bar. 4:19)*
Expectans expectavi — *Waiting, I waited (Ps. 39.1).*

48. FRACTIO

The 'Faith's fair symbol' of verse 25 refers to the repeated signs of the Cross made over the Host in the *Usus Antiquior* of the Roman Rite.

50. AFTER GOD'S HEART

The translation of the headings of this poem are, respectively: In the beginning; Countenance and Heart; Plentiful Bread; In the Night; At the End. In Part 4, the words *Eli, Eli, Lama Sabachthani* are those spoken by our Lord from the Cross in Matthew's account of the Passion and refer to the first verse of Ps. 21. It is translated as: *My God, my God, why hast thou forsaken me?* Following this, *Viriliter age* translates to: 'do manfully,' and refers to various passages in the Psalms (Ps. 26, Ps. 30), but more particularly to the passage in Judith that is used for the Offertory on the Feast of the Most Pure Heart of Mary: 'Because thou hast done manfully and strengthened thy heart, therefore the hand of the Lord has strengthened thee and thou shalt be blessed unto eternity' (Jdt. 15.11).

INDEX OF TITLES

ABOUT THE CENACLE PRESS
AT SILVERSTREAM PRIORY

An apostolate of the Benedictine monastery of Silverstream Priory in Ireland, the mission of The Cenacle Press can be summed up in four words: *Quis ostendit nobis bona* — who will show us good things (Psalm 4:6)? In an age of confusion, ugliness, and sin, our aim is to show something of the Highest Good to every reader who picks up our books. More specifically, we believe that the treasury of the centuries-old Benedictine tradition and the beauty of holiness which has characterised so many of its followers through the ages has something beneficial, worthwhile, and encouraging in it for every believer.

cenaclepress.com

ALSO AVAILABLE:

Robert Hugh Benson
The King's Achievement

Robert Hugh Benson
The Friendship of Christ

Dom Hubert Van Zeller OSB
We Work While the Light Lasts

Blessed Columba Marmion OSB
Christ the Ideal of the Monk

Blessed Columba Marmion OSB
Christ in His Mysteries

Blessed Columba Marmion OSB
Words of Life On the Margin of the Missal

Visit cenaclepress.com
for our full catalogue.

Lightning Source UK Ltd.
Milton Keynes UK
UKHW011240080722
405575UK00003B/831